P9-BTY-389

A Time to Choose

Tana Reiff

A PACEMAKER lifeTimes™ BOOK

GLOBE FEARON
Pearson

A Time to Choose

Tana Reiff
AR B.L.: 2.8
Points: 0.5

UG

LifeTimes™ Titles

Editorial Director: Robert G. Bander
Managing Designer: Kauthar Hawkins
Cover, text design, and illustrations: Wayne Snyder and
    Teresa Snyder

All characters herein are fictional. Any resemblance to real
persons is purely coincidental.

ISBN 0-8224-4322-8
Printed in the United States of America

7 8 9 10 11   06 05 04

Globe
Fearon

Pearson Learning Group

1-800-321-31
www.pearsonlearning.co

Contents

CHAPTER 1

Bob was going to race his car—
a Monza—
in the Fourth of July race.
It would be
his first time.
He had gone
to the races
for many years.
Now, at last,
he was going to be
in one.

Every day
Bob went right from
his job
to the garage.
He worked and worked
on his car.
On each run
he found something else
that needed to be fixed.

It took time,
but it was fun.
It would pay off
in a big way
if he won the race.

But Bob
worked so much that
he saw very little
of his wife, Jan.
Their girls, Ann and Kim,
were in bed
when he got home
at night.
He almost never saw them.

Most of the money Bob made
went into the car.
Jan had needed
a new washing machine
for a long time.
She never said anything
about it.
That was nice of her.
But it let Bob forget
that the need was there.

Bob loved
working on his car.
He loved fixing it.
He loved seeing it
shine in the sun.
He loved
showing it off
to his friends
at the garage.
Most of all,
he loved driving it.
Bob knew his Monza
was the best car
on the road.
He had made it
that way.
But it had cost him
a lot of time
and money.

Thinking It Over

1. What are your hobbies?
   Do they ever get in the way
   of other things
   in your life?

2. Do you spend money
   on your hobbies?
   What makes a hobby
   "worth it"?

3. If you were Jan,
   would you say anything
   about the time
   and money
   Bob spent
   on racing?

CHAPTER 2

The Fourth of July race
was only a week away.
Bob's car
was in good shape.
He was sure
he would do well.
But getting ready
took a lot of time.

So Bob started
calling in sick
to his job.
After three days
of calling in,
his boss got mad.
He said,
"OK, Bob.
We won't need you
any more."
It had happened.
He had been fired.

Bob had hated
his job.
He was glad
he had been fired.
It was no big deal.
He could win
the Fourth of July race.
He would get into
lots of other races
after that.
He would be the best.
He would love racing
as a full-time job.

But Jan
wasn't so happy
when Bob told her
he had lost his job.
She looked at him
with worry
on her face.
"Bob, what are we
going to do now?"
For the first time,
Jan told Bob
how she felt.

"Do you know
what your car
is doing
to me
and the kids?
We almost never
see you
any more.
You're always
working on your car
or at the track,"
Jan said.
"All your money
goes into
the car.
We don't even have
the clothes
we need.
And now—
where is the money
to live on
going to
come from?"

"But Jan,
I'm going to win

the Fourth of July race
for sure,"
Bob said.
"After that
I'll win other races.
Just wait and see.
Someday we'll be rich."

Thinking It Over

1. Do you think people
    should call in sick
    when they're not sick?

2. How would you feel
    if you lost a job
    that you hated?

3. What would it mean to you
    to be rich?

CHAPTER 3

It was
the Fourth of July.
Bob was ready
to race.
He hadn't been home much
the week before.
There had been a lot
to get ready for.
Jan and the girls
came to see Bob
in the race.

The Monza
was looking good
and running well.
Bob thought that
nothing could go wrong.
The car was in good shape.

Soon a man spoke
over the loudspeaker.

"Bring your cars
to the line!"
Bob was ready to go.

He was off!
His car was great.
He passed the other cars.
Bob was out in front.
He kept telling himself,
"I'm going to win!
I'm going to win!"
He drove faster and faster.
"Nothing can stop me now,"
he said to himself.

And then
something went wrong.
A back tire blew out.
At his speed
it was
a life or death matter.
Bob thought fast.
He took his foot
off the gas.
The car slowed down.
He could steer it.

He got the car
off to the side
of the track.
He was safe.
Bob had saved
his own life.

Those few seconds
had seemed like years.
Bob had never
used his head so well.
He saw now that
what people had told him
was true.
They said
if drivers
can act fast
when they need to,
they're pretty good drivers.

"I guess
I'm a pretty good driver,"
he told Jan that night.
"I'm lucky to be alive.
But, Jan,
I lost the race."

"Yes, Bob,"
said Jan.
"But you *are* alive."
She didn't care
that he had lost the race.
But she still wondered
where the money
would come from
to live on.

Thinking It Over

1.　Do you think
anything good can happen
without something going
wrong?
Why or why not?

2.　What should a driver do
if a tire blows out?

3.　When have you
had to think very fast?
Was it a matter of
life or death?

CHAPTER 4

Bob felt bad
about the Fourth of July race.
He spent
all of the next week
working on the car.
The Labor Day race
was coming up.
If he could
get the car ready,
he thought he could win.
But there wasn't
much time left.

Jan wasn't happy
that Bob was always
at the track.

"We're running out of money,"
she said.
"I think you
should get a job."

Bob had his mind
on the car—
not on the bills.
He asked Jan,
"Why don't *you*
get a job?"

"I didn't think
you wanted me to work,"
said Jan.

"It's different now,"
said Bob.
"This car
will start making money
real soon.
But we need money now.
You can keep us going
for a little while
if you work."

The last check
from Bob's old job
came and went.
So Jan looked
for a job.

She started working
as a clerk
in a men's store.
Kim and Ann
stayed with Jan's mother.

Bob spent his time
with the car.
The bills waited
for Jan's first paycheck.

Thinking It Over

1. If you were Jan,
   would you get a job?

2. What would you do
   if you had bills
   and no money coming in?

CHAPTER 5

Jan didn't like working
in the store.
She was tired
when she got home.
And the housework
still had to be done.

"Please, go back to work, Bob,"
she said.
"I can't work
in the store
and clean the house, too.
It's too much
for one person.
And besides,
we need to spend
more time
with the children.
I can't do everything
myself.
You have to help."

"I thought
you liked your new job,"
Bob said.

"At first I did,"
said Jan.
"But now I don't like working.
Please, Bob?"

"OK, OK,"
said Bob.
"Have it your way.
I'll sell the car.
I'll get a job.
But Jan—
I'm so sure I can make it.
Can't you try
to stick it out?"

Jan asked,
"Do you really think
you're going to win?"

"Yes, dear,"
said Bob.
"I really do."

"OK. I'll keep working,"
said Jan.
"But only until Labor Day.
If you don't win then,
I'll quit my job."

"It's a deal,"
said Bob.
"I'm sorry
I spend so much time
with the car.
But I really think
that I can win.
I really do.
And winning
the Labor Day race
would mean everything to us."

Thinking It Over

1. What does Bob mean
    when he says that
    winning the race
    means "everything"?

2. How can it help
    to talk to someone
    about a problem you have?

3. Do you think Bob and Jan
    made a fair deal?
    Why or why not?

CHAPTER 6

Labor Day
was a beautiful day.
The sun
looked like gold.
Bob thought
that was a good sign.

In the morning,
Jan took Kim and Ann
to the park
to swim
in the lake.
Bob went
to the track.
His car
looked good.
He was sure he could win.
He was in the last race
of the day.
Jan and the girls
came to see it.

This was it.
Win this race,
he thought,
and the day was his.
And the prize money, too.

He took his car
to the line.
At the start
of the race
he shot out
like a rocket.
So did the other cars.
They ran neck and neck.
Bob got in front.
Then another car
got in front.
Then Bob got a good lead.
Before he knew it,
it was over.
He had won!
What a day!

Jan and the girls
ran to meet Bob.
They were all happy.

Suddenly Bob had become famous.
Everyone
crowded around Bob
in the winner's circle.
The band
played music.
Everyone
talked at once
and shook Bob's hand.

Maybe Bob was right
after all,
Jan thought.
Maybe he *should*
be racing.

Thinking It Over

1. Do you believe
   that something can be
   a "good sign"?
   Why or why not?

2. Why do you think
   time sometimes goes fast
   and sometimes slowly?

3. Do you believe
   that hard work always
   pays off?
   Why or why not?

CHAPTER 7

The Labor Day race
was a big break
for Bob.
But he still spent
all his time
with the car.

Jan kept her job
at the store.
She was
not happy about it.
But they still needed
the money.
The prize money
went fast.
There was
a pile of old bills
to pay.
And it always took
a lot of money
to keep up the car.

Jan's job was
selling men's ties and shirts.
She didn't like it.
But she was very good at it.
She sold more
than anyone else
at the store.
And she was
learning a lot.

Her boss was
a man named Lou.
He thought
Jan was doing
a great job.
But he liked Jan
for more than that.
One day
he asked her out
to lunch.

Jan went to lunch
with Lou.
He was very nice to her.
He laughed
at her jokes.

He told her
she was a very smart woman.
Not even Bob
had said that
in years.
She was very taken
with Lou.
She began to forget
about her problems
at home.

Jan and Lou
went out for a drink
every day after work.
Sometimes they ate dinner together
When they did,
Jan would call her mother.
She would ask her
to give the kids dinner.
Her mother just thought
she was working late.

Kim and Ann
missed their parents.
They would ask their grandmother
"Where are Mommy and Daddy?"

Jan's mother
would always say,
"They are very busy, kittens.
They will kiss you tonight
when you're in bed."

"I really like you,"
Lou told Jan one night.
"It's too bad
you're married.
We could be
close friends."

Jan didn't know
what to say.
She *was* married.
She *did* have
two children.
But Lou—
well, he was
another world.

Lou went on.
"Your husband
doesn't spend much time
at home, does he?"

"No," said Jan.
"He races his car.
He says
he's going to
win a lot
of races."

Lou said,
"So he puts you to work
while he plays
with his car?"

"Kind of,"
said Jan.
"But I'm starting
to like work.
It's not so bad."

Lou asked another question.
"Have you ever thought
of leaving your husband?"

"Not really,"
said Jan.
"Until now."

Thinking It Over

1. What would you do
    if your husband or wife
    was never home?

2. Does Jan have
    a good reason to think
    about leaving Bob?

3. What do you think
    of someone who tells you
    how smart you are?

CHAPTER 8

One day
at the store,
Lou spoke to
Jan.

"I have something
to ask you,"
he said.

"OK,"
Jan said.

"Will you
come away
with me
to the lake
next weekend?
I want us
to get to know
each other
much better."

Jan asked,
"For the weekend?
I don't know.
What could I tell
my husband—
and the children?"

"Tell them
that you're going
to a company
sales meeting,"
Lou said.

Jan thought
about Lou's idea
for a few minutes.
Up to now
she had never thought
about having an affair.
Suddenly
it was happening.
Was it fair to Bob?
Maybe not.
But was Bob
being fair
to her?

Maybe it's time
for me
to see what
life is really like,
Jan thought.

"OK," she said.
"I'll work it out.
I'd like to go."

On Friday night,
Jan and Lou drove
to a small town
on the lake.
They ate dinner
by candlelight.
Then they sat
on the grass
and looked up
at the stars.
They talked
about many things—
about growing up,
about their school days,
about their families,
about themselves.

On Saturday
they visited
a famous flower garden.
They walked
in fields
of red and yellow and orange
flowers.

By breakfast
on Sunday,
Jan felt that
she had learned
a lot about Lou.
More important,
she had learned
a lot about herself.
She knew now
that this weekend
was not real.
It was too easy.
She and Lou
had left the real world
for a place where
there were no problems.
It was too easy
to run away

with someone
for a weekend of love.
But it was *hard*
to keep two people
together
when things were
going wrong.
That takes doing,
thought Jan.
That's what life is
all about.
Working out problems.
And you can't
run away
from that.
You always end up
taking the problems
along with you.

　　Driving home
that afternoon,
Jan turned
to Lou.
Then she said,
"Lou, it's been
a beautiful weekend.

You've been
so good to me.
And I hope
I've been good
for you.
But I think
we should stop
seeing each other."

   "I was afraid
you'd say that, Jan.
All day I've felt
you were moving away from me.
If that's how it is,
I'll stand back,"
Lou said.

Thinking It Over

1.   How important is it
     for people to try things
     they think they want to do?

2.   Does it help or hurt people
     to tell them
     your real feelings?

CHAPTER 9

Bob left
the track
early Friday afternoon.
He had been thinking
about what
Jan had told him.
He hadn't seen
much of her
or the children
lately.
Maybe his racing *was* getting
out of hand.
Anyway,
the car was
in good shape.
So Bob thought
he would go home
and do some
of the housework.
That would show Jan
that his heart

was in the right place
after all.

   At home,
Bob washed the dishes.
Then he cleaned
the whole house.
By six o'clock
Jan still wasn't home.
Then the telephone rang.
It was Jan's mother.

   "Jan asked me
to call you,"
she said.
"She couldn't reach you
at the track.
She's going out of town
to a sales meeting
until Sunday.
I'm keeping the girls
here with me
for the weekend."

   "Thanks, Mother,"
Bob said.

He hung up.
Then he thought,
A sales meeting?
That's the first time
I've heard of it.

   At dinner time
on Sunday,
Jan came home.

   "Hello, Bob,"
she said.
"Are the children
still with my mother?"

   "Yes," Bob said.
"But why didn't
you tell me sooner
that you were going off?
Where have you been?"

   "You haven't seemed to be
at all interested
in what I'm doing,"
Jan said.
"I wasn't even sure

that you would know
I was gone."

"Really?
Is that so?
It might
surprise you to know
that I came home
Friday afternoon
to help you
clean the house,"
Bob said.

Jan looked at him.
"Have you ever heard
the saying,
'Too little, too late'?"

"*Is* it
too late, Jan?
I came
to help Friday
because I *know*
I haven't been
fair to you,"
Bob said.

"You haven't been fair.
But I haven't either.
I should have
told you myself
that I was going away."

Bob moved
across the room
and reached for
Jan's hands.
She put her hands
in his.

"Bob," said Jan.
"Let's make
a decision
together.
Both of us.
Let's promise
always to be fair
to each other,
no matter what."

Bob let go
of Jan's hands.
He smiled.

He put his arms
around her.

"I want
to make that decision
with you, Jan.
Now.
For good."

Jan asked,
"You don't think
racing will
come between us
again?"

"I won't let it,"
Bob said.
"And one other thing
I won't do.
I won't ever worry
that you will be
unfair to me
again."

Thinking It Over

1. Does it help
   to talk things out?

2. Should Jan have told Bob
   that she went away
   with Lou for the weekend?

CHAPTER 10

Lou had helped Jan
look at things
in a new way.
She had loved going out
with him.
It was nice
to hear how great she was.
But she loved Bob.
Now she knew it
for sure.
She would try her best
to keep things together.
It wouldn't be easy.
But she would try.
She still wished
there was more money
coming in.

She didn't see Lou again.
She got a job
in a different store.

Bob never knew why
she changed jobs.
Jan would never tell him.

Winter was
on its way.
Bob was getting
his car ready
for the first race
of the spring.
One day
while Bob was working
on his car
he got a telephone call
from Jan.

"Joe Silva called,"
said Jan.
"He wants to talk to you
about a job."

"A job?
This *is* my job,"
said Bob.
"We will be fine
if I keep on winning."

"Yes, Bob,"
said Jan.
"If you keep on winning.
But what if you don't?
I don't make
enough money.
Please call Joe.
I think it might be
a good thing.
It could be
a long, hard winter."

"OK, OK.
I'll call
and see what he has
to say."

Bob hung up the phone.
Then he called Joe Silva.

Thinking It Over

1. Do you think
   that a family man
   should have a full-time job?
   Why or why not?

2. Do you think
   it's important
   to always feel safe
   from money problems?
   Why or why not?

CHAPTER 11

Joe and Bob
had been friends
for a long time.
Joe ran a big garage
in town.
He could fix any car
and do a fine job.
What did he
have in mind for Bob?

"Hi, Joe.
This is Bob.
What's up?"

"Hi, Bob!
I called to tell you
that I need
a new head mechanic,"
Joe said.
"A good one.
I know you don't have

a job right now.
I want you
to work for me.
I need you, Bob.
How about it?"

Bob didn't say a word
for a minute.
"Boy, Joe,
I don't know.
I've been spending
all my time
on my car.
I wasn't even thinking
about a full-time job."

"Think it over, Bob,"
said Joe.
"You're good.
You're a good driver
and a good mechanic.
But you're taking chances.
And you know
your family needs
more from you
than just chances.

I'm sorry,
but that's what I think."

   "I'll think it over.
I'll call you back
in the morning."
Bob said good-bye
and hung up.
Well, well, he thought.
I have some thinking to do.

Thinking It Over

1. Do you ever
   "speak your mind"?

2. Do you take chances
   in your life?
   Does it help you
   or hurt you?

3. If you were Bob,
   would you take the job?
   Why or why not?

CHAPTER 12

Bob didn't want
to tell Jan anything
until later.
He knew
Joe was right.
But what about the races?
What about his car?
What about
all his hard work?
The really big drivers
were the ones
who took a lot of chances.
And if they made it,
they made it big.
That's what Bob wanted.
But was it worth
what was going on now?
Could he pay the price?
He had to think
of all sides
of the problem.

Then he would talk
to Jan about it.

Bob thought about
his problem
as he walked
back to his car.
When he got there,
a man was waiting
to talk to him.
The man asked,
"Are you the one
who runs this car?"

"Right. My name is Bob."

"Hi. I'm Jim Ross.
I'd like to sponsor you."

"What? Really?
Be my sponsor?"
Bob was so happy
he didn't know
what to say.
What a break!
This was just

what he had wanted
for so long.
If someone else
would pay for the car,
his problems
would be over.

"Yes, Bob,"
said Jim Ross.
"I want to sponsor you.
Of course,
you have to be a winner.
You must be good,
or I can't keep
paying for you."
The man told Bob
about the deal
he wanted to make.

Joe Silva and the job in town
were gone from Bob's mind.

Thinking It Over

1. How do you go about
    making up your mind?

2. Why is it so easy
    to forget something
    you don't want to think
    about?

3. Would you take Jim's job?
    Would you take Joe's job?

CHAPTER 13

"Jan!
Wait until you hear this!
A man named Jim Ross
wants to be my sponsor,"
Bob said.
"We're all set, kid!"

Jan gave him
a little smile.
"That's nice,"
she said.
Then she asked,
"What did Joe Silva
have to say?"

"Oh,"
said Bob.
"He wants
to give me a job
as his head mechanic.
But, Jan, who needs that

when I can race
and not think
about the money?"

"Bob, we both know
it's not that easy,"
Jan said.
"There's a lot more to it
than that.
Have you made up your mind,
or can we talk about it?"

Bob didn't know
what to say.
He had promised
to be fair to Jan.
But now
he was very mixed up.
It had been so clear to him
until he talked
to her.
If he kept the car
and got a sponsor,
he would be in good shape.
That is,
if he kept on winning.

If he took the job—
well, there were good points
about both sides.

Sometimes you just have to
make up your mind,
Bob thought.
He had an OK life now.
What would he do with it
from now on?

"Let's go out
to dinner, Jan,"
said Bob.
"Let's talk."

"OK," said Jan.
"The kids are at Mom's.
Let's go."

They got their coats
and walked out the door.
They had a lot
to talk about.
The time
had come

for an important decision
to be made.
But this decision
would be made
together.

Thinking It Over

1. Are there two sides
   to every question?
   Why or why not?

2. Did you think of
   other people
   when you made big decisions?

3. What would you do
   if you were Bob?
   If you were Jan?